Roxy's Life
with **Ophthalmic Brainstem Glioma**

By: Roxanne Lugar

Compiled Dialogue and Art:
Kimberly Leighton, MS, CCLS

ISBN:
978-1-63308-750-7 (paperback)
978-1-63308-751-4 (ebook)

Cover and Interior Design by *R'tor John D. Maghuyop*

CHALFANT ECKERT
PUBLISHING

PO Box 1665, Rolla MO 65402

Printed in United States of America

Roxy's Life

with Ophthalmic Brainstem Glioma

By: Roxanne Lugar

Compiled Dialogue and Art:
Kimberly Leighton, MS, CCLS

Dedication

I am dedicating this book to my foster parents, "Mom" and "Dad" (Michelle and Peter), my child life specialist, Kim, and also my Mimi and Papa, Mom Mom and Pa, Dr. Chaleff, and Braden, another play warrior author that inspired me to write my own book.

Me, Mom, and Dad

**Me and Kim
at Play Warriors**

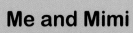

Me and Mimi

Me and Dr. Chaleff
At Maine Children's Cancer Program

Hi my name is Roxanne and I am 8 years old and I am in the third grade.

I live in Maine with my foster parents, Mom and Dad.

Me at my 8th birthday party

We have two mini donkeys named Sonar and Blue,
a hairless cat named Jezabell, and two dogs
named Indica and Mac.

Mac is our new puppy.

Painting of (acrylic on canvas)

Blue and Sonar

I am writing this story to help other kids learn about
the type of cancer that I have. It is called
ophthalmic brainstem glioma.

I just learned how to say it! It is a very long name.
I am legally blind and can't see like other kids do.
I am learning Braille and I have a cane that
I named, Rosie May, to help me walk.

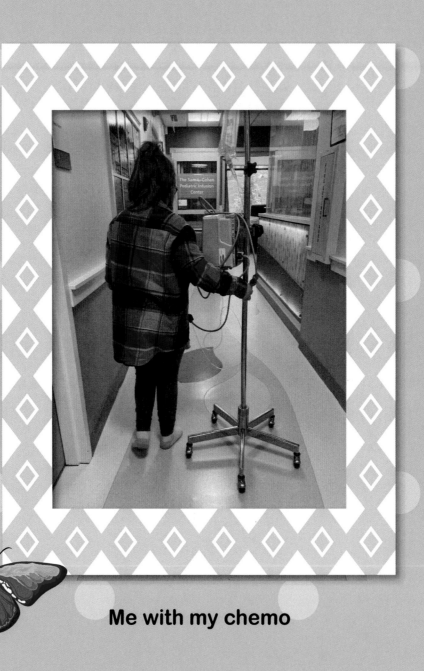

Me with my chemo

When I was five years old I didn't feel good.
I was having night terrors. It felt like someone
was punching me in the back of my head.

One day, my Mimi drove me to the hospital and we
went to a place called Maine Med. I remember
I was crying because I was in so much pain.

That is when I found out I had cancer.

"Mimi and Me at the Hospital" Mixed media on canvas

The nurses and doctors were nice and they helped me.
They placed an IV in the middle of my arm to
give me medicine and I fell asleep.

An IV is a needle that gives you medicine into your
blood. The nurse puts cream on and it feels numb.
Then you feel a quick pinch and it is all done.

Me at the hospital

When I was asleep, I had my brain biopsy.
A brain biopsy is when the doctor opens up your
head and takes a piece of your brain.

After, they closed it and glued it back together.
Because I was asleep, I couldn't feel it.
When I woke up, my head hurt and it was wrapped
up. I liked having my Mimi by my side.

A few weeks later I had to have another brain biopsy.

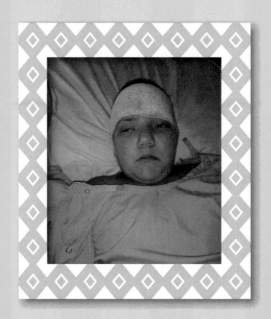

Me after my brain biopsy

Me with my brain

Chemo is the medicine that helps my cancer go
away. For a little while, I was off chemo. It was fun.
I didn't have to worry about when I ate.

But I had to go back on chemo and get another port in
my chest to get a new type of medicine. I have to get
infusions every week for four hours. Sometimes I color
and watch the Ipad and hang out with Mom and Dad.

I feel mad that I have to be back on chemo.
It's okay to feel mad.

Me getting my chemo infusion

I love going on adventures with my family.

We went to Disney and had so much fun!

My favorite part was going on all of the rollercoasters.

Me. Mom, and Dad

One place that I would love to go
and have never been is Dollywood because I love
Dolly Parton. I even dressed up as her for Halloween.

I have Dolly pajamas, a Dolly cup, and a Dolly baking kit too!

One day I hope to meet Dolly Parton.

Me dressed up as Dolly Parton for Halloween

Even though I have cancer, I am setting goals for myself.

I decided to get baptized at my church and everybody came.

I wanted to get baptized because I want to be
God's daughter, and when it is my turn to
turn to God, I want to see him.

Me getting baptized

Most days I go to school and
I like to do everything at school, especially math!
I just changed schools and it is going good so far.

I also get to go to Play Warriors for child life therapy
and I get to see the therapy bunny, "Caramel Cookie".
Sometimes I get to take him for a walk.

Me and Caramel Cookie

Over the past weekend, my vision got worse.
It is gone and I cannot see anything.

When this happened I felt worried and upset.

I am feeling depressed.

Me releasing a butterfly

I want to tell other kids with cancer that you
have to keep fighting and never give up.

The way I handle it is just to try to forget about
it, and focus on the good things.

My family keeps me going and my friends help me at school.

My wish is for all kids with cancer to get better.

I really love my family, and I want them to know
I am always going to be with them forever.

And we all lived happily ever after.

The End.

Final hand casting

Thank you to these organizations:

 Boston Children's Hospital

Made in the USA
Middletown, DE
14 October 2024

62604685R10024